MW01125739

Trademark Like A Boss

The Ultimate Step-By-Step Guide
to Protecting Your Brand

Radiance W. Harris, Esq.

Trademark Like A Boss: The Ultimate Step-By-Step Guide to Protecting Your Brand/ Radiance W. Harris, Esq.

ISBN 978-1-7358274-0-7 (Paperback)

ISBN 978-1-7358274-1-4 (eBook)

This book is a resource for educational and informational purposes, does not constitute legal advice, and should not replace hiring an attorney. This book also creates no attorney-client relationship between you and Radiance Harris or Radiance IP Law.

Scan the QR code below or visit
radianceiplaw.com/bookfreebie to download your free copy
of the Trademark Like A Boss Tools & Resources guide.

I dedicate this book to my exceptional husband, Johnnyrhette, and my precious son, Josiah, whose selfless love, support, and patience has kept me inspired throughout my legal career and book-writing journey.

To my dad, mom, sister, and grandma, thank you for always praying for me, supporting my crazy dreams, and encouraging me to shine brighter.

This is only the beginning.

Contents

Table of Figures

"A U.S. federal trademark registration is essentially like a birth certificate for your business."

Introduction

Imagine this: You started your business in 2018. At that time, you did not protect your business name with a trademark. You just opened your business and started using the name. A couple years later, business is booming. You're exceeding your income goals. Then, you find out that someone has literally copied your name and started offering competitive products or services.

Of course, you're pissed because you're almost certain they copied you. You dig further and discover that the copycat business started using your exact business name in 2019, a year after you started using it, and also secured a U.S. federal trademark registration for the name, but you did not. Now, you're not able to trademark the name because a competitor already did, and there isn't really anything you can do.

Trademark protection isn't just for major corporations. Startup and emerging businesses need trademarks too. While working at a major global law firm early in my career, I regularly sent nasty grams (also known as cease and desist letters) on behalf of Fortune 200 companies to protect and enforce their trademark rights.

The receivers of those nasty grams were often entrepreneurs and small business owners. For some reason, entrepreneurs and small businesses were not aware of or did not understand the importance of trademark protection. This experience inspired me to start my own law firm, Radiance IP Law, a few years ago, and to write this book so I could help small and emerging businesses protect their brands just like the major corporations do.

In 2018, over 640,000 trademark applications were filed in the United States.[1] Of course, this number includes both small and large businesses that understand the immense value and importance of trademark ownership.

Trademark protection is neither a fad nor a trend. It is also not a task that you just leave on your to-do until whenever you arbitrarily decide to make the investment. It

---

1 WIPO Statistics Database, March 2020

is an essential part of establishing legal ownership and protection of your brand and business, creating a unique marketing edge, standing out in a crowded and competitive marketplace, avoiding expensive legal disputes and lawsuits, preventing brand theft or misuse, and providing peace of mind to grow your business and increase profits.

What Is A Trademark?

A trademark or service mark is a word, phrase, symbol, or design, or any combination of these, that serves as a source identifier for your products and services, and distinguishes your products or services from those of your competitors. Trademarks may include:

- Words (STARBUCKS)
- Slogans (IT'S FINGER LICKIN' GOOD)
- Letters and numbers (ABC or 747)
- Sounds (NBC Chime)
- Symbols (McDonald's Golden Arches)
- Colors (Tiffany Blue)
- Shape (Hershey's chocolate bar)
- Motion (Lamborghini's scissor doors)
- Scents (Play-Doh scent)

To illustrate, when you see or hear "Nike" or "Just Do It," you immediately think of the famous footwear and apparel brand. Similarly, when you see the Apple logo, you immediately think of the famous technology company and the high-quality products that they create and sell.

But, here's the thing. These companies weren't always large and famous. Just like you, these companies started out small – in their basement, garage, or two-bedroom apartment, but they secured their trademarks at the very beginning to prepare and protect themselves for their future business vision and growth.

A trademark serves a major purpose not only for businesses but also for consumers in the marketplace. It helps consumers differentiate your products or services from those of your competitors. Trademarks and service marks serve the same purpose and can be referred to collectively as trademarks or marks. A trademark is typically used to identify and distinguish products from each other. A service mark is used to identify and distinguish services from each other.

In addition to trademarks and service marks, there are also certification and collective membership marks. A certification mark is used by others to certify that they have met the standards or specifications of the certifying body. A great example is the ENERGY STAR certification, which certifies to the public that certain items meet the highest standards for energy efficiency as defined by the U.S. Environmental Protection Agency.[2]

When purchasing a refrigerator or light bulb, you'll often see that ENERGY STAR certification, which gives you assurances that the product has met the established energy-saving standards.

Figure 1: Energy Star Certification

A collective membership mark is owned by a collective of members to a group or organization to identify and distinguish their goods and services from non-members and to indicate their membership in the group. A great example is the collective membership mark used by members of the National Association of Realtors.

---

2 ("ENERGY STAR | The Simple Choice for Energy Efficiency." n.d.)

Figure 2: National Association of Realtors Membership Designation

The National Association of Realtors does not sell products or services under this mark, but instead, advertises and promotes the products or services of its members. In this book, I will primarily cover trademarks and service marks, but I wanted you to be aware of these other types of trademarks.

Why Is Trademark Protection Necessary?

Trademarks provide tremendous value to both businesses and consumers. A trademark allows businesses to distinguish themselves from the competition so that consumers can easily find them and make quick, confident, and safe purchasing decisions.

A trademark also conveys a message about your products and services, and your company as a whole. It helps your prospective clients and customers decide whether or not they want to spend their money purchasing from your business.

To illustrate further, imagine walking into a grocery store to purchase shampoo. As you walk down the shampoo aisle, you notice all of the shampoo bottles are white with black letters on the front with the word, "Shampoo." How does a consumer make a decision about which shampoo is the best for them to buy if they all look the same? There are no distinguishing brand elements.

Now, consider this scenario if you're a service-based business. Imagine driving down a major street to find a hair salon, and you come across five buildings with a sign on the front with the words, "American Hair Salon." How does a potential client make a decision about which hair salon to patronize? The purpose of a trademark is to make it easy for your prospective clients and customers to find you and your products and services.

Trademarks are valuable property assets for your business with actual monetary value. This asset can be sold, licensed, or transferred, just like real estate. Trademarks increase the value of your brand and business, which is especially important if you ever decide to sell or transfer your business or obtain capital from investors. In addition, trademarks prevent brandjackers and copycats from benefiting from the brand recognition and reputation you've built, and allow you to pursue legal action with harsh penalties against any infringers.

Contrary to popular belief, neither your LLC filing, domain name, nor social media handles give you any trademark rights or protection. There are only two ways to establish trademark rights and protection in the United States.

The first and most limited way to establish trademark rights is through use. If you are simply using your business name, product or service name, slogan, and/or logo in connection with your products or services without a U.S. federal trademark registration, you can only claim common law trademark rights. This essentially means you only have rights to use the name in a limited geographic region.

For example, if you have a coaching business based in New York but have been offering your coaching services to clients in New York and throughout the United States, you can only claim trademark rights in New York and prevent theft in New York. You would not be able to prevent a competitor from using an identical or similar business name to yours in Pennsylvania, for example, or any other state.

If you've been operating your business without any U.S. federal trademark registrations, you have, at the very least, common law trademark rights in your state and the limited ability to prevent trademark infringement by a competitor in your state.

The second and most comprehensive way to establish trademark rights is by obtaining a federal trademark registration from the U.S. Patent and Trademark Office. Once you obtain U.S. federal trademark registrations for your business name, product or service name, slogan, and/or logo, you will have the exclusive right to use your name, slogan, and/or logo in your industry in all 50 states and prevent your competitors from using them or anything similar.

A U.S. federal trademark registration confers numerous benefits. These benefits include:

1. Nationwide rights as of the application filing or priority date
2. Automatic presumption of legal ownership
3. Right to use the ® symbol
4. Ability to license the use of your content and products to others
5. Ability to assign or sell your trademark rights to others
6. Enhanced remedies for infringement (treble damages, costs, and attorney's fees)
7. Protection against the importation of counterfeit goods

As such, a U.S. federal trademark registration is essentially like a birth certificate for your business.

The Key Phases of the Trademark Process

From start to finish, the U.S. federal trademark registration process takes, on average, one year. To secure a U.S. federal trademark, there are 5 key phases:

1. Naming your business, products, and services
2. Properly identifying the trademarks you can and should protect in your business
3. Conducting a search to determine that your proposed trademark(s) are available for your use and registration in the United States
4. Executing the trademark application process with the U.S. Patent and Trademark Office
5. Maintaining and enforcing your rights as a trademark owner

The purpose of this book is to successfully guide you step-by-step through the U.S. federal trademark registration process. My goal is to empower and equip you with the tools to protect the brand and business of your dreams and... trademark like a boss. By protecting your brand, you are demonstrating to yourself and others that you believe in your brand and the success of your business.

An Important Disclaimer

This book is a resource for educational and informational purposes, does not consti-tute legal advice, and should not replace hiring an attorney. This book also creates no attorney-client relationship between you and Radiance Harris or Radiance IP Law.

"Naming your business isn't like naming your child."

Chapter One
The Anatomy of a Fireproof Name

Not all names are viewed or treated equally.

In fact, 72% of the best brands are made-up words or acronyms[3] and 77% of consumers make purchases based on a brand name.[4] A distinctive business name allows you to stand out from your competition. A distinctive name is a profitable name. In addition, distinctive names are most protectable as trademarks.

Your name should create an original image in your prospective client or customer's head similar to these distinctive brand names: KLEENEX, GOOGLE, CBS, NBC, ESPN, XEROX, DELL, LEXUS, TOYOTA, NISSAN, ADIDAS, and PUMA.

Choose and use a name that you love, is memorable, is easy to pronounce, tells a story about and connects to your brand, and will differentiate your products and/or services from all of the other businesses that do exactly what you do. Those are the best names.

Marketers and trademark attorneys usually butt heads when it comes to naming etiquette because marketers usually say to choose a name that describes your business, but trademark attorneys say to choose a unique name that sets you apart. Naming your business isn't like naming your child. You shouldn't just come up with a name that you like and roll with it, without any additional considerations or research.

The more your business, product, or service name conveys about the nature of your products or services, the weaker it is, and the less likely it will get granted a trademark. When naming your business, product, or service, there are 5 distinctiveness levels you should consider.

---

3 ("50+ Eye-Opening Branding Statistics - 2020 Edition" 2019)
4 ("The Ultimate Guide to Choosing a Brandable Name for Your Startup • Domain.Me Blog" 2018)

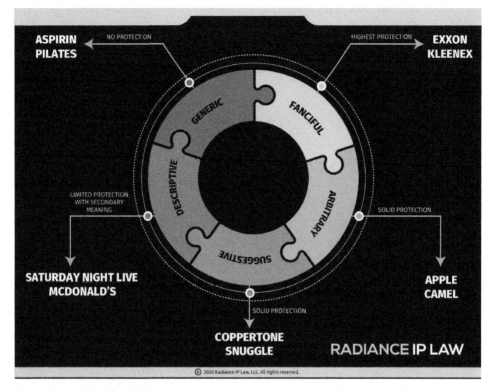

Figure 3: Levels of Distinctiveness

The most (inherently) distinctive names are invented words (also known as fanciful marks). Examples of fanciful marks include GOOGLE and KLEENEX. These names are the best types of business, product, or service names from a trademark protection standpoint.

The second level consists of names derived from words in the English dictionary that are applied to unrelated products and services (also known as arbitrary marks). Examples of arbitrary marks include APPLE, for computers and mobile devices, and CAMEL for cigarettes. These names are also great options from a trademark protection standpoint.

The third level consists of names that require an additional leap in the minds of consumers to determine the nature of the products and services (also known as suggestive marks). Examples of suggestive marks include COPPERTONE for sun care products (which suggests the copper color of your skin when you apply their products) and SNUGGLE for fabric softener (which suggests the soft and cuddly feeling

24

of your clothing after using their products). These names are good options from a trademark protection standpoint.

The fourth and least distinctive level consists of names that describe a feature or characteristic of your products and services (also known as descriptive marks). These names are only protectable as trademarks after demonstrating acquired distinctiveness or secondary meaning.

To achieve acquired distinctiveness or secondary meaning, you must have at least five years of exclusive and continuous use of your descriptive name in connection with your products or services in commerce.[5]

Personal names can be descriptive. MCDONALD'S, SATURDAY NIGHT LIVE, and CAPITAL AREA FOOD BANK are considered descriptive names, but each acquired distinctiveness and became protected trademarks. As a best practice, stay away from descriptive names.

The lowest level without any distinction are names that categorize and define a type of product or service (also known as generic marks). ASPIRIN, ESCALATOR, and PILATES are considered generic and are not eligible for trademark protection. It's a great idea to avoid generic names when naming your business, products, and services.

If you are struggling with naming or have not chosen a name yet, here's a quick and effective process that you can use. Do a 5-minute brain dump:

1. Grab a pen and paper and set your timer for 5 minutes.
2. On the next page, write down each and every word that comes to mind when you think about your brand message, your products, your services, your mission, your deliverables, your process, your benefits, your solutions, your results, and how you want your clients or customers to feel after purchasing your products or services.
3. No words are off-limits. Just let them all spill out on paper without any thought, judgment, or edits.
4. At the end of those 5 minutes, you should have a long list of words, at least 25 - 30.

---

5 ("How to Claim Acquired Distinctiveness under Section 2(f) | USPTO" n.d.)

5. Start highlighting any words that really stand out to you (or ask a very close friend or family member to do so) and see what you can come up with.

6. Develop at least 5 name ideas so that you have options to consider and narrow down, if necessary. Your name ideas might be only one of the listed words, a combination of a couple of words, or a newly invented word inspired by your list. The more creative you get, the better. The goal is to give yourself the opportunity to develop a handful of decent name ideas.

NAME IDEAS

"1 out of 3 small businesses rebrand due to trademark similarity, but that doesn't have to be your story."

Chapter Two
Research Like Your Business Depends On It... Because It Does

The next (most important, yet often neglected) step is to conduct a trademark search prior to adopting a name for your business. The primary reasons for searching are to:

- Research the competition
- Obtain valuable business information
- Determine availability for use
- Determine availability for registration
- Determine the strength and scope of protection
- Help you understand and accept potential risks
- Help you plan for contingencies
- Avoid unnecessary legal disputes
- Avoid loss of your investment
- Avoid awards for damages, lost profits, and attorney's fees to someone for infringing on their trademark
- Pay a little now or a lot more later

Failing to conduct a trademark search before adopting the use of a name can lead to expensive, time-consuming, and stressful legal disputes and overall rebrand. It costs you much less when you're proactive instead of reactive. The best times to search are:

- Before adoption and first use of a name
- Before brand extensions
- Before licensing to others
- Before expanding geographically within or outside of the United States

However, before you jump into the trademark search, you need to first identify the names you're using or considering and the products and services that you are currently selling and/or planning to sell under each name.

There are rules to what you can and can't trademark. I didn't write them, but it's my duty to make sure that you understand them. For example, you may trademark the following:

- Business name
- Product name(s)
- Service name(s)
- Slogan
- Logo
- Icons
- Hashtags
- Event name(s)
- Blog name(s)
- Podcast name(s)
- Course name(s)

If a name is functioning as a source identifier for your products and/or services, then it is eligible for trademark protection, provided that it is distinctive (as discussed in the prior chapter) and not infringing on someone else's prior trademark rights (as discussed in the next chapter).

On the flip side, there are certain things that you just can't trademark. To illustrate, for example, you cannot trademark the following:

- Generic terms or phrases
- Informational messages
- Widely used messages
- Bible passages
- A geographic location
- Single book, song, or movie titles
- Famous names or likenesses without consent from the person

- Government symbols or insignia
- Deceptive words or symbols

Here are examples of trademarks based on industry:

Coaches, Consultants, and Therapists

- Business name
- Program name(s)
- Podcast name
- Book series name
- Blog name
- Logo
- Slogan

Health and Wellness

- Business name
- Fitness program name(s)
- Product name(s)
- Logo
- Slogan

E-Commerce

- Online store name
- Product name(s)
- Logo
- Slogan

Food

- Business name
- Food product name(s)
- Logo
- Slogan

Computer Software/Mobile Application

- Business name
- Software name(s)
- App icon(s)
- Logo
- Slogan

Now that you better understand what you can and can't trademark, it's important to clearly identify your potential trademarks along with your current or intended products and/or services for each trademark before moving forward with the trademark application process. You should identify any names, phrases, or logos that you're currently using or planning to use within the next 12 to 18 months. In addition, you should identify any products and services that you're currently selling and planning to sell within the next 12 to 18 months.

For example:

Trademark	Current Products/Services	Future Products/Services
RADIANCE IP LAW (business name)	Legal services	N/A
RADIANCE IP LAW (business logo)	Legal services	N/A
TRADEMARK LIKE A BOSS (product name)	Trademark course Trademark book	Podcast
THE TRADEMARK BOSS (service name)	Legal services	N/A

Figure 4: Example Products and Services

Identify Your Trademarks

Now, it's your turn to take a moment to identify each trademark along with your current and future products and services. Here's a quick tip: be overinclusive (instead of underinclusive) when identifying your products and services for each potential trademark. As discussed in a later chapter, once you file your trademark application with the U.S. Patent and Trademark Office ("USPTO"), you cannot add any product or services to the application. You can only narrow or delete products and services. To add any new products or services, you must file an entirely new trademark application with the USPTO.

Trademark	Current Products/Services	Future Products/Services

For each of the products and services that you've identified, you'll want to determine their correct classification with the USPTO.

Correctly identifying your products and services is a crucial step in the U.S. trademark application process. The USPTO has organized products and services according to specific categories or classes.

You must file your application under the appropriate class. In some cases, you might need to register your trademark in more than one class to accurately cover your products and/or services. Additional filing fees are required for each trademark class. There are 45 trademark classes, with 34 product categories and 11 service categories.

Product Classifications

Class No.	Type	Description of Goods[6]
Class 1	Chemicals	Chemicals for use in industry, science, and photography, as well as in agriculture, horticulture, and forestry; unprocessed artificial resins, unprocessed plastics; fire extinguishing and fire prevention compositions; tempering and soldering preparations; substances for tanning animal skins and hides; adhesives for use in industry; putties and other paste fillers; compost, manures, fertilizers; biological preparations for use in industry and science
Class 2	Paints	Paints, varnishes, lacquers; preservatives against rust and against deterioration of wood; colorants, dyes; inks for printing, marking and engraving; raw natural resins; metals in foil and powder form for use in painting, decorating, printing, and art
Class 3	Cosmetics and Cleaning Preparations	Non-medicated cosmetics and toiletry preparations; non-medicated dentifrices; perfumery, essential oils; bleaching preparations and other substances for laundry use; cleaning, polishing, scouring and abrasive preparations

6   ("Headings of International Trademark Classes, TMEP § 1401.02(a), October 2018" n.d.)

Class 4	Lubricants and Fuels	Industrial oils and greases, wax; lubricants; dust absorbing, wetting and binding compositions; fuels and illuminants; candles and wicks for lighting
Class 5	Pharmaceuticals	Pharmaceuticals, medical and veterinary preparations; sanitary preparations for medical purposes; dietetic food and substances adapted for medical or veterinary use, food for babies; dietary supplements for humans and animals; plasters, materials for dressings; material for stopping teeth, dental wax; disinfectants; preparations for destroying vermin; fungicides, herbicides
Class 6	Metal Goods	Common metals and their alloys, ores; metal materials for building and construction; transportable buildings of metal; non-electric cables and wires of common metal; small items of metal hardware; metal containers for storage or transport; safes
Class 7	Machinery	Machines, machine tools, power-operated tools; motors and engines, except for land vehicles; machine coupling and transmission components, except for land vehicles; agricultural implements, other than hand-operated hand tools; incubators for eggs; automatic vending machines
Class 8	Hand Tools	Hand tools and implements, hand-operated; cutlery; side arms, except firearms; razors

Class 9	Electrical and Scientific Apparatus	Scientific, nautical, surveying, photographic, cinematographic, optical, weighing, measuring, signaling, checking (supervision), life-saving and teaching apparatus and instruments; apparatus and instruments for conducting, switching, transforming, accumulating, regulating or controlling electricity; apparatus for recording, transmission or reproduction of sound or images; magnetic data carriers, recording discs; compact discs, DVDs and other digital recording media; mechanisms for coin-operated apparatus; cash registers, calculating machines, data processing equipment, computers; computer software; fire-extinguishing apparatus
Class 10	Medical Apparatus	Surgical, medical, dental and veterinary apparatus and instruments; artificial limbs, eyes and teeth; orthopedic articles; suture materials; therapeutic and assistive devices adapted for the disabled; massage apparatus; apparatus, devices and articles for nursing infants; sexual activity apparatus, devices and articles
Class 11	Environmental Control Apparatus	Apparatus for lighting, heating, steam generating, cooking, refrigerating, drying, ventilating, water supply and sanitary purposes
Class 12	Vehicles	Vehicles; apparatus for locomotion by land, air, or water
Class 13	Firearms	Firearms; ammunition and projectiles; explosives; fireworks
Class 14	Jewelry	Precious metals and their alloys; jewelry, precious and semi-precious stones; horological and chronometric instruments
Class 15	Musical Instruments	Musical instruments

Class 16	Paper Goods and Printed Matter	Paper and cardboard; printed matter; bookbinding material; photographs; stationery and office requisites, except furniture; adhesives for stationery or household purposes; drawing materials and materials for artists; paintbrushes; instructional and teaching materials; plastic sheets, films and bags for wrapping and packaging; printers' type, printing blocks
Class 17	Rubber Goods	Unprocessed and semi-processed rubber, gutta-percha, gum, asbestos, mica and substitutes for all these materials; plastics and resins in extruded form for use in manufacture; packing, stopping and insulating materials; flexible pipes, tubes and hoses, not of metal
Class 18	Leather Goods	Leather and imitations of leather; animal skins and hides; luggage and carrying bags; umbrellas and parasols; walking sticks; whips, harness and saddlery; collars, leashes, and clothing for animals
Class 19	Non-metallic Building Materials	Building materials (non-metallic); non-metallic rigid pipes for building; asphalt, pitch, and bitumen; non-metallic transportable buildings; monuments, not of metal
Class 20	Furniture and Articles Not Otherwise Classified	Furniture, mirrors, picture frames; containers, not of metal, for storage or transport; unworked or semi-worked bone, horn, whalebone or mother-of-pearl; shells; meerschaum; yellow amber
Class 21	Housewares and Glass	Household or kitchen utensils and containers; cookware and tableware, except forks, knives and spoons; combs and sponges; brushes, except paintbrushes; brush-making materials; articles for cleaning purposes; unworked or semi-worked glass, except building glass; glassware, porcelain and earthenware

TRADEMARK LIKE A BOSS

Class 22	Cordage and Fibers	Ropes and string; nets; tents and tarpaulins; awnings of textile or synthetic materials; sails; sacks for the transport and storage of materials in bulk; padding, cushioning and stuffing materials, except of paper, cardboard, rubber or plastics; raw fibrous textile materials and substitutes therefor
Class 23	Yarns and Threads	Yarns and threads, for textile use
Class 24	Fabrics	Textiles and substitutes for textiles; household linen; curtains of textile or plastic
Class 25	Clothing	Clothing, footwear, headgear
Class 26	Fancy Goods	Lace and embroidery, ribbons and braid; buttons, hooks and eyes, pins and needles; artificial flowers; hair decorations; false hair
Class 27	Floor Coverings	Carpets, rugs, mats and matting, linoleum and other materials for covering existing floors; wall hangings (non-textile)
Class 28	Toys and Sporting Goods	Games, toys and playthings; video game apparatus; gymnastic and sporting articles; decorations for Christmas trees
Class 29	Meats and Processed Foods	Meat, fish, poultry and game; meat extracts; preserved, frozen, dried and cooked fruits and vegetables; jellies, jams, compotes; eggs; milk and milk products; oils and fats for food
Class 30	Staple Foods	Coffee, tea, cocoa and artificial coffee; rice; tapioca and sago; flour and preparations made from cereals; bread, pastries and confectionery; edible ices; sugar, honey, treacle; yeast, baking-powder; salt; mustard; vinegar, sauces (condiments); spices; ice (frozen water)

x

Class 31	Natural Agricultural Products	Raw and unprocessed agricultural, aquacultural, horticultural and forestry products; raw and unprocessed grains and seeds; fresh fruits and vegetables, fresh herbs; natural plants and flowers; bulbs, seedlings and seeds for planting; live animals; foodstuffs and beverages for animals; malt
Class 32	Light Beverages	Beers; mineral and aerated waters and other non-alcoholic beverages; fruit beverages and fruit juices; syrups and other preparations for making beverages
Class 33	Wine and Spirits	Alcoholic beverages (except beers)
Class 34	Smokers' Articles	Tobacco; smokers' articles; matches

Figure 5: Product Classifications

Service Classifications

Class No.	Type	Description of Services[7]
Class 35	Advertising and Business	Advertising; business management; business administration; office functions
Class 36	Insurance and Financial	Insurance; financial affairs; monetary affairs; real estate affairs
Class 37	Building Construction and Repair	Building construction; repair; installation services
Class 38	Telecommunications	Telecommunications
Class 39	Transportation and Storage	Transport; packaging and storage of goods; travel arrangement

---

7 Id.

Class 40	Treatment of Materials	Treatment of materials
Class 41	Education and Entertainment	Education; providing of training; entertainment; sporting and cultural activities
Class 42	Computer and Scientific	Scientific and technological services and research and design relating thereto; industrial analysis and research services; design and development of computer hardware and software
Class 43	Hotels and Restaurants	Services for providing food and drink; temporary accommodation
Class 44	Medical, Beauty & Agricultural	Medical services; veterinary services; hygienic and beauty care for human beings or animals; agriculture, horticulture and forestry services
Class 45	Personal	Legal services; security services for the physical protection of tangible property and individuals; personal and social services rendered by others to meet the needs of individuals

Figure 6: Service Classifications

All products and services registered by the USPTO are categorized into one of these classes. You should not categorize under the class headings alone because the classes itself are too broad. Instead, you must specify certain items under the classes you wish to protect. The USPTO has a listing of acceptable descriptions of goods[8] and services, known as the Trademark ID Manual[9] as shown here.

---

8 The U.S. Patent and Trademark Office uses the term "goods" to identify products.

9 ("Headings of International Trademark Classes, TMEP § 1401.02(a), October 2018" n.d.)

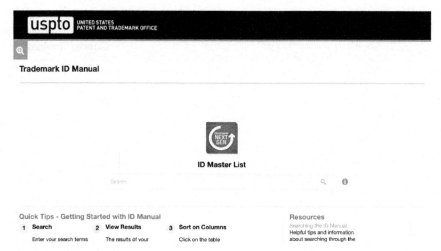

Figure 7: Trademark ID Manual

Go to this manual and type in each of your products and services to determine the correct description and trademark class.

One of the most common mistakes is choosing the wrong class when completing a trademark application.[10] Doing so can result in the denial of your trademark application, requiring you to start over and pay new (additional) application filing fees.

You should take your time to research the Trademark ID Manual and carefully identify the correct description and trademark class. You can also hire an experienced trademark attorney to identify the correct classes and descriptions for your trademark(s).

For example, if you sell business coaching or consulting services, you may search "business coaching" or "business consulting." The search may reveal hundreds of descriptions to choose from. You should identify the description that best describes your services, along with its corresponding trademark class. Similarly, if you sell t-shirts, you should type into the search box, "shirts," and then identify the best description and trademark class.

You may use this chart to write down the description of goods and services and trademark class for each potential trademark based on your research in the Trademark ID Manual.

---

10 To avoid this mistake, it is best to hire an experienced trademark lawyer to identify the right classes and accurate descriptions for your trademark(s).

Trademark	Trademark Class	Acceptable Description of Goods/Services

Once you've clearly identified your potential trademarks along with the correct trademark class and description of goods and services, you're ready to conduct a trademark search.

How to Conduct a Trademark Search

To conduct a trademark search, you will research the USPTO database, the Internet, and domain names. To be clear, this search is not nearly as thorough or comprehensive as the searches typically conducted by an experienced trademark attorney, but it will help you eliminate any bad names before you commit. To minimize confusion or overwhelm, it is best to tackle one name at a time.

There are 3 key components to a trademark search:

1. U.S. Patent and Trademark Office search
2. Common law search
3. Domain name search

You'll start with the U.S. Patent and Office database, called the Trademark Electronic Search System (TESS), which is available at **tmsearch.uspto.gov**. A TESS search should help determine whether your name is available for use and registration in the United States.

Be sure to search direct matches, similar matches (including obvious/plural variations), obvious misspellings/sound-alikes/alternate spellings, and English translations (if it's a foreign word). For example, if your business name is Radiance IP Law (I'm sure it's not, but just humor me), you may search variations, "radience" and "radiant."

It's best to start with the New User Search to see if there are any direct hits. If the search pulls up only a handful of records (let's say, less than 30), you should go through each of them to see if any of the trademarks cover the classes or goods and/or services that apply to your business. If the search pulls up too many records (let's say, more than 100), you can use the Free Form Search to narrow down the search based on the trademark class(es) and/or goods and services.

As you're conducting the search, write down any potential red flags. Generally speaking, identical names are red flags. If you come across any nearly identical or similar names on the Federal Register covering any classes along with any products and/or services that apply to your business, it's probably not a good idea to move forward, and your search ends there.

If, however, you did not come across any red flags, you should conduct a further search to see if there are any businesses that may have prior common law trademark rights. A common law trademark means that the business hasn't federally registered their trademark yet, but are actively using it to sell products and/or services. Their prior use gives them common law trademark rights in a certain limited geographic area. A common law search includes the following:

1. Secretary of State's business records (in each state your business has a presence)
2. The Internet, using Google and other search engines
3. Social media websites
4. Amazon
5. Domain names

As before, jot down any red flags.

When reviewing your search results as a whole, you should ask yourself these questions:

1. Is the name protectable as a trademark? (Specifically, is it distinctive based on the continuum discussed in Chapter One?)
2. Is the name available for **use** in the United States? (Specifically, is there a competition with prior trademark rights?)
3. Is the name available for **registration** in the United States? (Specifically, is there a prior U.S. federal trademark application or registration for an identical or similar name in my industry?)

When considering whether you may be committing trademark infringement, ask the question:

Would my potential clients or customers be confused or misled by my use of a competitor's identical or similar trademark?

It's called the likelihood of confusion standard. Carefully review your search results and determine whether you're safe to proceed with your desired name(s). If you're too close to a competitor's trademark, and they find out about it, you could receive a nasty gram and, even worse, get sued for trademark infringement with harsh penalties and damages. Also, the USPTO may refuse registration of your trademark based on a likelihood of confusion with a prior application or registration. The reality is that 1 out of 3 small businesses rebrand due to trademark similarity, but that doesn't have to be your story.

So, what's considered too close for comfort? Here are examples of trademarks found to be confusingly similar:

- QUEENDOM AESTHETICS & Design for beauty creams, beauty lotions, beauty milks, and make-up vs. QUEENDOM for beauty creams, beauty lotions, beauty milks, and make-up
- LIQUOR SLINGER DISTILLING for liquor vs. SLINGER for drinking glasses and shot glasses
- WIZGEAR for electronic accessories vs. THE WIZ and NOBODY BEATS THE WIZ for retail services for electronic accessories and equipment
- MAUNA KEA RUM COMPANY for spirits and rum vs. MAUNA KEA & Design for restaurant services
- RUFF CHEWERS for dog and pet toys vs. RUFF CHEW for pet beds
- ACTTRA for agricultural insecticides vs. ACTARA for agricultural insecticides
- CUBNOXIOUS for shirts vs. CUBS for shirts
- TEMPUS for beer vs. TEMPUS TWO for wines
- DAILY FILL for retail store services featuring convenience store items and gasoline vs. DAILY'S for retail store services featuring convenience store items and gasoline

You should be aware that there are professional databases and online vendors that conduct trademark searches. However, these third-party databases and vendors tend to be expensive, complicated, and/or provide too much information to decipher and understand. You can also hire an experienced trademark attorney to conduct a comprehensive trademark search. An attorney can also review the search results and recommend whether you should attempt to trademark a name.

"Prepare and file your trademark application as soon as possible, but certainly within 48 hours of doing your own search."

Chapter Three
Prepare the Application

Once the search reveals that your proposed name is available for use and registration in the United States, the next step is to prepare your trademark application with the USPTO. The search results become obsolete as time passes; therefore, it's best to prepare and file your trademark application as soon as possible, but certainly within 48 hours of doing your own search.

You can file a trademark application on your own, but because the process can be time-consuming, confusing, overwhelming, and expensive, you may consider hiring an experienced trademark attorney. Hiring a trademark attorney is not as intimidating as you may think, and increases your chances of securing a trademark registration by over 60%.

Assuming you prefer to take the DIY route, you must prepare a separate trademark application for each name or logo. You'll need to determine whether you're filing for a word mark or a design mark. You can file to register for either:

- Standard characters (word mark in block letters); or
- Special form (stylized and/or design mark)

It is best to file in standard characters when you're not claiming a particular font style, size, and/or color. It is best to file in special form when your trademark includes a design or words combined with a design or is displayed in a particular font style, size, and/or color.

If you have a limited budget, I would suggest starting with a filing for standard characters (a word mark in block letters) because it gives you the broadest trademark protection in all variations. You can only file one trademark per application. Therefore, if you have a word mark and a design mark, you'll need to file the word mark in one application and the design mark in a separate application.

Here are examples of the different filing types:

Standard Characters	Special Form
RADIANCE IP LAW	
RAREGLO	
MONEY WITCH	
AWESOME WOMEN	
NUBOXX	
B.O.O.S.T.	
THE NEXT DIRECTION IN SOLAR	
THE BRANDING BABE	

Figure 8: Examples of Trademark Filing Types

There are two ways to file the trademark application:

- Based on current use under Section 1(a)
- Based on an intent to use under Section 1(b)

If you've already been using a name or logo on products and/or services in the marketplace and can provide evidence of that use, then you should file based on current use. If you have not been using a name on products or services yet, but have a "bona fide intention to use the mark in commerce"[11] within the next year or two, then you should file based on an intent to use.

Filing the trademark application based on your intent to use in the near future is a great way to stake your claim to a specific name before adoption and use. It's also a way to ensure that the name you wish to use is actually available to register before you start posting it all over signage and marketing and advertising materials.

When filing based on an intent to use, however, you must submit evidence of actual trademark use to the USPTO within at least 1 to 3 years of the application filing date before you can obtain a registration.

If you know that you're going to launch a new business, product, or service within the next year or so, then you should file based on an intent to use so that you can claim rights to use the name before someone else beats you to it while you're getting your business plans and affairs together.

Filing based on an intent to use allows you to claim priority as of the application filing date. Once you actually start using and register the trademark, you can enforce your rights against any subsequent users or application filers.

When filing based on current use, you will need the following to complete the trade-mark application:

- Trademark applicant/owner's name
- Mailing address and email address for correspondence
- For a special form filing, a clear JPG image of the stylized or design mark and a written description of the mark
- A description of the goods and services (as discussed in Chapter Two)
- The date of first use of the mark anywhere and the date of first use of the mark in interstate commerce in connection with the applied-for goods and services
- Evidence showing use of the mark in connection with the applied-for goods or services (also known as a specimen of use)
- USPTO filing fees (the fee is per application per class)[12]

---

11 ("TMEP § 1101 (Bona Fide Intention To Use the Mark In Commerce)." n.d.)
12 Check the USPTO website for the current filing fees ("Trademark Fee Information | USPTO" n.d.)

When filing based on an intent to use, you will need the following to complete the trademark application:

- Trademark applicant/owner's name
- Mailing address and email address for correspondence
- For a special form filing, a clear JPG image of the stylized or design mark and a written description of the mark
- A description of the goods and services (as discussed in Chapter Two)
- USPTO filing fees (the fee is per application per class)[13]

Trademark Application Tips

Here are a few trademark application tips to simplify the process:

- Because a trademark is a business asset, it is best to file the application with your business entity (LLC or corporation) listed as the trademark applicant/owner.
- Use your residential or business address as the mailing address on your application.[14] The official trademark registration will be mailed to the address on file. If you move or change your address during the application process, be sure to update the USPTO with your new address. All information in your trademark application becomes a part of the public record and is searchable in the USPTO database and through a Google search.
- Use the email address that you use and check regularly. All correspondence and updates from the USPTO will be sent to your email address.
- If you're filing for a stylized or design mark, you should consider filing in black and white (as opposed to color) for broader protection and flexibility. In this case, you will need to upload a clear black and white (or grayscale) JPG image for the stylized or design mark with your application. The image must contain very little white space around the design as possible. If you're claiming color as a feature of your mark, submit the image in color using the RGB color scheme.
- "Date of first use in trade" means the date of the mark's first use anywhere. "Date of first use in commerce" means the date of the mark's first use in interstate commerce. "Interstate commerce" means any commerce that Congress can regulate, such as interstate commerce, commerce involving U.S. Territories, commerce with

---

13 *Id*.
14 ("TMEP § 803.05 (Address of Applicant)" n.d.)

other countries, or territorial commerce in Washington, D.C., or with Indian tribal reservations/nations. It is a very broad definition and includes selling to customers who cross state lines (such as out-of-state visitors to a local establishment), and shipments across state lines are considered interstate commerce. Commerce that is entirely local within one state or locality within a state is not interstate commerce. The two dates can be the same, or, if a business was entirely local at first and then expanded to interstate, they could be two different dates. Provide the earliest dates of first use possible for each trademark class in the application.

- If you're filing based on an intent to use, you will submit the dates of first use and trademark use evidence later in the process for an additional filing fee (the fee is per application per class). You should check the USPTO website to confirm the current filing fees.

Acceptable evidence of trademark use is essential to obtaining a trademark registration. If filing based on current use, you must submit your trademark evidence (or specimen of use) when filing the trademark application.

If filing based on a bona fide intent to use, you will submit your trademark evidence (or specimen of use) a few months later in the application process. In either case, to be acceptable for trademark registration purposes, your trademark evidence must show the actual mark as used in commerce in the sale or advertising of the applied-for goods or services in the United States.

You will need to provide evidence for each class you apply for. For example, if you file for t-shirts under Class 25 and on-line retail store services under Class 35, you must submit evidence of the actual t-shirt product and the online retail store website.

Here are examples of acceptable evidence of trademark use for goods and services:

GOODS	SERVICES
• A photograph of the product showing the mark directly on the product • Product labels and tags showing the mark • Product packaging showing the mark • Signage used in a product display at a store • A website screenshot showing or describing the product(s) near the mark and with purchasing information (including URL and the date you accessed or printed the webpage) • For downloadable software, copies of the instruction manual and screen printouts from (1) webpages showing the mark in connection with ordering or purchasing information or information sufficient to download the software, (2) the actual program that shows the mark in the title bar, or (3) launch screens that show the mark in an introductory message box that appears after opening the program	• Print or Internet advertising • Brochures and leaflets • Menus for restaurants • Business cards and letterhead • Marketing and promotional materials • Photograph of business signage or billboards • Photograph of a musical band performing with the band's name displayed during the performance • A website screenshot showing or describing the service(s) near the mark (including URL and the date you accessed or printed the webpage)

Figure 9: Acceptable Evidence of Trademark Use for Goods and Services Examples

As shown, there are items that may qualify as acceptable trademark use evidence for goods, but not for services, and vice versa. Therefore, you should make sure that you are submitting the correct type of evidence with your trademark application. You should also submit the evidence to the USPTO in JPG or PDF format.

Here are a few illustrations of acceptable trademark use evidence that you may submit with your trademark application.

For Goods

(Body Butter in Class 3)

Figure 10: Acceptable Evidence of Trademark Use in Class 3 Example

(Publications in Class 16)

Figure 11: Acceptable Evidence of Trademark Use in Class 16 Example

(Shirts in Class 25)

Figure 12: Acceptable Evidence of Trademark Use in Class 25 Example

For Services

(Fitness studio services in Class 41)

Figure 13: Acceptable Evidence of Trademark Use in Class 41 Example

(Internet-based health care information services in Class 44)

Figure 14: Acceptable Evidence of Trademark Use in Class 44 Example

(Legal services in Class 45)

Figure 15: Acceptable Evidence of Trademark Use in Class 45 Example

For goods, you may submit a photograph of the product, displaying the applied-for trademark being used in connection with the identified goods in the application. For services, you may submit a photograph of your storefront or a website screenshot displaying the applied-for trademark being used in connection with the identified services in the application. You simply must prove to the USPTO that you're actually using the trademark exactly as you've applied for it.

Use this simple checklist to gather the information you need to file your trademark application.

TRADEMARK APPLICATION PREP CHECKLIST

☐ The trademark you wish to protect

☐ Trademark applicant/owner name

☐ Mailing address

☐ Email address

☐ If filing for a special form (stylized/design mark), a clear image of the stylized or design mark

☐ If filing for a special form (stylized/design mark), a written description of the mark

☐ A description of all goods and services currently offered or intended to be offered under the trademark

☐ The basis for filing the trademark application: current use <u>or</u> intent to use

☐ If filing based on current use, the date of first use anywhere <u>and</u> date of first use in interstate commerce for the trademark in connection with the identified goods and/or services above

☐ If filing based on current use, evidence of current trademark use for the identified goods and/or services above

☐ USPTO application filing fees

"Expect the U.S. trademark registration process to take, on average, about 10 months to 1 year, or longer."

Chapter Four

File the Application

We've finally gotten to the "meat and potatoes," which is actually filing your trademark application with the USPTO. As much as I would love to explain every single thing you need to know about trademark law and the entire application process, that level of specificity and education requires a full-blown law degree and an extensive career in trademark law.

Of course, I will do my absolute best to simplify this process as much as possible for you and prepare you for the potential hurdles that you may face along the way. Sound good?

You should expect the U.S. trademark registration process to take, on average, about 10 months to 1 year, or longer.

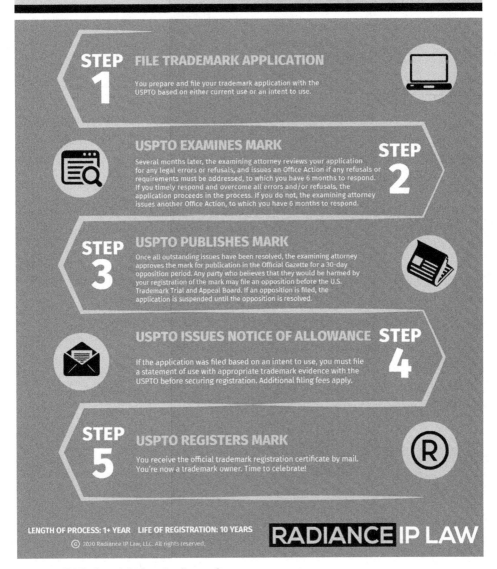

Figure 16: U.S Trademark Registration Process Summary

Of course, during this lengthy process, you may continue with your business affairs. You do not have to wait until the registration process is complete before you start using your trademark.

During the process, you can use the ™ symbol next to your trademark to alert competitors and would-be infringers of your plans to register with the USPTO. However, to be clear, the ® symbol is the only legal designation that truly matters and carries actual legal weight.

To file the trademark application online, use the TEAS online filing system, which is located at teas.uspto.gov. Go to the initial application forms and start your trademark application in TEAS. The most cost-effective and streamlined filing option is TEAS PLUS. It's best to use this form. If you're unable to find a listing that accurately describes your goods and services in the Trademark ID Manual (which is a requirement for TEAS PLUS), then you must use the TEAS Standard filing option.

Carefully follow the instructions on the online form and provide all of the requested information (as previously outlined in Chapter Three). Once you've completed the trademark application and submitted the online form, you must pay the filing fees.

After submitting payment, you will receive confirmation of your application filing via email. If, for some reason, you did not receive an email confirmation, you probably either entered your email address incorrectly or did not successfully submit the application along with payment.

Roughly 3 months after filing your trademark application, a trademark examining attorney from the USPTO will examine your trademark application and issue an Office Action if there are any outstanding issues in the application that need to be addressed, to which you have 6 months to respond. About 70% of applications receive an Office Action, which is a preliminary denial. In an Office Action, an examining attorney can raise procedural issues or more complex substantive refusals.

Procedural issues may include:

• Required amendments to the identification of goods and services
• Required substitute specimen
• Disclaimers
• Requests for more information

More complex substantive refusals may include:

• Likelihood of confusion
• Descriptiveness

- Deceptive material
- Geographically descriptive
- Geographically deceptively misdescriptive
- Geographically deceptive
- Merely a surname
- Does not function as a trademark

For the procedural issues, you can probably address them on your own. If anything is unclear, pick up the phone and call your assigned examining attorney to gather more information about what you need to respond to the Office Action.

For more complex substantive refusals, however, you should absolutely consult with and hire an experienced trademark attorney (wink, wink - her name is Radiance) before responding. You should not try to respond to these refusals on your own.

These substantive refusals often require a lengthy legal brief response with case law citations and exhibits, which involves a clear understanding of U.S. trademark law and strong persuasive legal writing skills.

It would be flat out awful for you to miss out on getting your trademark application approved by failing to respond to the Office Action or responding incorrectly because you did not know what you were doing. Sadly, you'll also lose out on your application filing fees, which are non-refundable.

Once you've resolved all outstanding issues in any Office Actions, your trademark will be published for opposition in the Official Gazette for 30 calendar days. During this time, anyone who believes that they will be harmed by your registration of the trademark can file an opposition before the U.S. Trademark Trial and Appeal Board.

A trademark opposition is an administrative proceeding that challenges your ability to register a trademark. It does not, however, affect your ability to use a trademark. If your trademark application is opposed, this is another part of the application process where you should consult with and hire an experienced trademark attorney.

If no opposition is filed for a use-based application, the USPTO will issue the registration. If no opposition is filed for an intent-to-use application, the USPTO will issue a notice of allowance, and you will have 6 months to file a Statement of Use or request an extension of time.

You have roughly 2.5 years from the Notice of Allowance date to file the Statement of Use before your trademark application goes abandoned. In other words, you can file up to a total of five 6-months extensions.

Once you've commenced use of the applied-for trademark in interstate commerce, you should file the Statement of Use with the appropriate trademark evidence and dates of first use, as discussed in Chapter Three. Once the USPTO accepts the Statement of Use, it will issue the registration.

The USPTO will mail an official registration certificate to the address on file in your trademark application. Once this happens, you're officially a trademark owner!

"Let's pop champagne (or sparkling apple cider, if that's your thing)!"

Chapter Five
You're a Trademark Boss

Congratulations, Trademark Boss! Once your trademark is registered with the USPTO, and you have the certificate in hand, you're official. And guess what? You should be super proud because ownership is king. Here are a few important responsibilities you shouldn't take lightly as you embark on your journey as a trademark owner:

Marking: Use of ® Designation

Use the ® designation each time you use your trademark. For example, Radiance IP Law®. You may only use the registration symbol with the mark on or in connection with the goods/services listed in the U.S. federal trademark registration.

If you start using the registered mark in connection with goods/services that are not covered in the U.S. federal trademark registration, or a mark which has not been registered yet, use the TM or SM designation to indicate your common law use and adoption of the name, logo, or slogan until you pursue registration.

What's the difference between the ™ and ® symbols?

TM	®
You only have common law trademark rights in your state, based on use.	You have a U.S. federal trademark registration from the U.S. Patent and Trademark Office.
You have no nationwide rights or protection.	You have legal ownership along with exclusive nationwide rights and protection.
You have no (or very limited) recourse against infringement and theft.	You have legal recourse against infringement and theft.
You have a potential threat of receiving a cease and desist letter and/or a lawsuit.	You have a distinctive brand from your competitors and peace of mind to grow your business.
You cannot license, sell, or transfer.	You have a valuable business asset that you can license, sell, or transfer just like real estate.

Figure 17: Comparison of Common Law and Registered Trademark Designations

Maintaining Your Trademark

To maintain your trademark registration, you must file your first maintenance document between the 5th and 6th year after the registration date.

Your registration certificate contains important information on maintaining your federal trademark registration. If the documents are not timely filed, your registration will be cancelled and cannot be revived or reinstated, making the filing of a brand-new application to begin the overall process again necessary. Forms for filing the maintenance documents are found at teas.uspto.gov.

Rights in a federally registered trademark can last indefinitely if you continue to use the mark and file all necessary maintenance documents with the required fee(s) at the appropriate times, as identified below.

The necessary documents for maintaining a trademark registration are:

- Declaration of Continued Use or Excusable Nonuse under Section 8 (§8 declaration); and

- Combined Declaration of Continued Use and Application for Renewal under Sections 8 and 9 (combined §§8 and 9 declaration)

A §8 declaration is due before the end of the 6-year period after the registration date or within the 6-month grace period thereafter. Failure to file this declaration will result in the cancellation of the registration.

A combined §§8 and 9 declaration must be filed before the end of every 10-year period after the registration date or within the 6-month grace period thereafter. Failure to make these required filings will result in the cancellation and/or expiration of the registration.

Monitoring and Enforcing Your Trademark Rights

To maintain exclusive ownership of your federally registered trademark, under U.S. trademark law, you are now responsible for policing and enforcing your trademark rights against any infringing third parties. When you invest money and resources to protect your brand, the last thing you want is someone stealing it.

Throughout the life of the registration, you must police and enforce your rights. Any unauthorized use or misuse of your trademark(s) should not be ignored. You have a duty to police and enforce unauthorized use and misuse or risk losing your trademark rights.

Trademark infringement arises when two separate and unrelated companies engage in the use of identical or similar trademarks for identical or similar products and services, resulting in actual or potential consumer confusion.

While the USPTO will block any subsequent application for an identical or similar mark used on identical or similar goods or services from proceeding to registration based on a likelihood of confusion, the USPTO will not engage in any separate policing or enforcement activities.

You should regularly monitor the USPTO website and the Internet for any potential violations. Be sure to include all trademarks in Google Alerts so that you're notified whenever your trademarks are mentioned on the Internet. You should also become familiar with the infringement reporting policies and procedures on all major social media platforms.

If you suspect trademark infringement, contact an experienced trademark attorney (hint, hint - her name is Radiance) to research the merits of your alleged claims, recommend the best course of action, and possibly send a cease and desist letter on your behalf.

Beware of Trademark Scams

Several companies attempt to profit by sending notices that appear to be official and offering unnecessary services to trademark applicants and registrants whose information they obtain from the U.S. Patent and Trademark Office website. Do not assume that any such invoices or service offerings from third parties are legitimate. Be suspicious of any invoices or documents that require you to pay inflated fees, even if they claim to be required by law.

These solicitations and notices can be intimidating to the untrained eye because they often reference an agency that appears to be the USPTO and your application or registration number. Don't be bamboozled! You will only receive official correspondence concerning your trademark application or registration only from the U.S. Patent and Trademark Office, which is located in Alexandria, Virginia. Always read documents carefully before you respond. Visit the official "Non-USPTO Solicitations" webpage at https://www.uspto.gov/trademarks-getting-started/non-uspto-solicitations for more information about and examples of non-USPTO solicitations.

Trademark Do's and Don'ts

DO'S	DON'TS
• Use your trademark as an adjective (i.e., use a XEROX copier, not XEROX these copies)	• Adopt a name, logo, or slogan without first conducting a search
• Be consistent and display your mark the same way each time	• Use similar or identical names to third parties in the same or related field, or famous brands
• Use ® to claim federally registered trademark or service mark rights in the U.S. (i.e., RADIANCE IP LAW®)	• Use third party logos in your advertising and marketing materials without the owner's prior consent
• Always display your mark in a different font or manner from surrounding text in printed material (i.e., APPLE® computer or Kleenex® tissues)	• Use your trademark as a noun (i.e., book a flight on JETBLUE today) or a verb (i.e., please XEROX this document)
	• Fail to update ownership information with the USPTO
	• Forget to ensure all information in the registration is accurate
	• Use the ® designation in connection with any unregistered trademarks or any goods or services not included in your trademark registration(s)
	• Fall victim to trademark scams

Figure 18: Trademark Do's and Don'ts

With trademark ownership comes the priceless peace of mind to grow your brand and business, and focus on what you truly love and do best... go forth and conquer. To celebrate, let's pop champagne (or sparkling apple cider, if that's your thing)!

"U.S. trademark registrations are of tremendous value to your business."

Conclusion

Whether your goal is to distinguish yourself from the competition, grow a million-dollar brand, secure money from investors, license your intellectual property to others for income, expand your brand globally or from one industry to another, or sell your business as part of a succession plan or major acquisition, U.S. trademark registrations are of tremendous value to your business.

Now more than ever, it is extremely important not to delay trademark protection. Even if your business is mostly local, if you have a website and social media presence and engage in online advertising, you're creating a global digital footprint, exposing your brand to potential infringement, theft, misuse, and legal disputes.

As shown, the U.S. federal trademark registration process takes, on average, about 10 months to a year, and sometimes even longer. If you start the process now, you'll hopefully have a shiny U.S. trademark registration certificate in hand by this time next year.

Each time you delay just a few months, you are pushing back the time before you can proudly proclaim, "I'm a Trademark Boss." Of course, once you do complete the U.S. federal trademark registration process, I hope you will credit this book for your success.

Tools and Resources

Important Trademark Links

U.S. Patent and Trademark website: https://www.uspto.gov/

Search pending and registered marks: http://tmsearch.uspto.gov/

File applications and other documents online: https://www.uspto.gov/trademarks-application-process/filing-online

Check application status/view or download trademark records: http://tsdr.uspto.gov/

Check U.S. Trademark Trial and Appeal Board records: http://ttabvue.uspto.gov/ttabvue/

Check trademark fees: https://www.uspto.gov/trademark/trademark-fee-information

Trademark Like a Boss Worksheet

Use this worksheet to take notes and reference as your step-by-step guide during the U.S. trademark registration process.

CHAPTER ONE – THE ANATOMY OF A FIREPROOF NAME

For trademark protection, your name must be distinctive. There is a spectrum of distinctiveness, which determines the degree of protection for a certain name. The distinctiveness spectrum includes (in order of most to least distinctive):

1. **Fanciful names** consist of invented or made-up words that do not exist in any dictionary and are inherently distinctive, making them excellent for trademark protection.

2. **Arbitrary names** consist of real words applied to unrelated goods or services and are registrable as trademarks.

3. **Suggestive names** suggest a quality or characteristic of the goods or services and are registrable as trademarks.

4. **Descriptive names** describe the product or service, use the owner's name, or indicate the geographic location of a product or service. These names aren't registrable as trademarks without a showing of acquired distinctiveness or secondary meaning.

5. **Generic names are** the actual name of the products or services and are not registrable as trademarks.

Where does your name fall on the distinctiveness spectrum?

If you have not chosen a name yet, do the 5-minute brain dump exercise to develop fireproof name ideas.

CHAPTER ONE NOTES

CHAPTER TWO – RESEARCH LIKE YOUR BUSINESS DEPENDS ON IT...BECAUSE IT DOES

☐ Identify your trademark(s)

☐ Identify your offerings (goods and services)

☐ Use the Trademark ID Manual to determine the trademark classes and appropriate descriptions of goods and services for your offerings

Conduct the trademark search:

☐ USPTO Search

☐ Internet Search

☐ Domain Name Search

☐ Write down any red flags

☐ Review the trademark search results

☐ Determine whether your trademark is available for use and registration in the United States

CHAPTER TWO NOTES

CHAPTER THREE - PREPARE THE APPLICATION

☐ Determine the type of mark you are filing for: (1) standard characters (word mark in block letters); or (2) special form (stylized and/or design mark)

☐ Determine your filing basis for the trademark application: (1) current use; or (2) intent to use

FILING BASED ON CURRENT USE – Requirements:

☐ Trademark applicant/owner's name

☐ Mailing address and email address for correspondence

☐ For a special form filing, a clear image of the stylized or design mark and a written description of the mark

☐ A description of the goods and services

☐ The date of first use of the mark anywhere and the date of first use of the mark in interstate commerce in connection with the applied-for goods and services

☐ Evidence showing use of the mark in connection with the applied-for goods or services (also known as a specimen of use)

☐ USPTO filing fees (the fee is per application per class)

FILING BASED ON INTENT TO USE – Requirements:

☐ Trademark applicant/owner's name

☐ Mailing address and email address for correspondence

☐ For a special form filing, a clear image of the stylized or design mark and a written description of the mark

☐ A description of the goods and services

☐ USPTO filing fees (the fee is per application per class)

ACCEPTABLE TRADEMARK EVIDENCE

Goods

- A photograph of the product showing the mark directly on the product
- Product labels and tags showing the mark
- Product packaging showing the mark

- Signage used in a product display at a store

- A website screenshot showing or describing the product(s) near the mark and with purchasing information

- For downloadable software, copies of the instruction manual and screen printouts from (1) webpages showing the mark in connection with ordering or purchasing information or information sufficient to download the software, (2) the actual program that shows the mark in the title bar, or (3) launch screens that show the mark in an introductory message box that appears after opening the program

Services

- Print or Internet advertising

- Brochures and leaflets

- Menus for restaurants

- Business cards and letterhead

- Marketing and promotional materials

- Photograph of business signage or billboards

- Photograph of a musical band performing with the band's name displayed during the performance

- A website screenshot showing or describing the service(s) near the mark

CHAPTER THREE NOTES

CHAPTER FOUR - FILE THE APPLICATION

1. Go to **teas.uspto.gov**
2. Click on the initial application forms and start your trademark application in TEAS PLUS
3. Follow the instructions on the online form
4. Complete and submit online form
5. Submit payment for filing fees
6. Receive confirmation from USPTO via email

HOW TO HANDLE OFFICE ACTIONS

(Deadline to Respond: 6 Months)

For the procedural issues, you can probably address them on your own. If anything is unclear, pick up the phone and call your assigned examining attorney to gather more information about what you need to respond to the Office Action.

For more complex substantive refusals, however, you should absolutely consult with and hire an experienced trademark attorney (wink, wink - her name is Radiance) before responding. You should not try to respond to these refusals on your own.

HOW TO HANDLE AN OPPOSITION

A trademark opposition is an administrative proceeding that challenges your ability to register a trademark. It does not, however, affect your ability to use a trademark. If your trademark application is opposed, this is another part of the application process where you should consult with and hire an experienced trademark attorney.

CHAPTER FOUR NOTES

CHAPTER FIVE – YOU'RE A TRADEMARK BOSS

☐ Use the ® designation

☐ Calendar your post-registration maintenance filing deadlines

☐ Make proper and consistent trademark use

☐ Monitor for infringement

☐ Enforce your trademark rights against infringers

CHAPTER FIVE NOTES

BONUS NOTES

Trademark rights are jurisdictional. Some countries are first-to-use; other countries are first-to-file. There are two ways to file internationally: **(1)** Madrid Protocol; or **(2)** file directly in the countries of interest using local counsel. Contact an experienced trademark attorney for assistance with international filings.

BONUS NOTES

Trademark Cease and Desist Letter Template

Radiance IP Law, LLC created this basic template. It is not one-size-fits-all. You will need to edit this template and tailor it to your specific situation before use. Guidance notes and highlights throughout will help you get started. During the editing process, you should delete those guidance notes and highlights. If you have any questions or concerns about the editing or use of this template, seek professional legal advice from an experienced trademark attorney.

This basic template is a resource for educational and informational purposes, does not constitute legal advice, and should not replace hiring an attorney. This template also does not create an attorney-client relationship between you and Radiance Harris or Radiance IP Law.

Date

Infringer's Name
Company Name (if applicable)
Mailing Address
City, State Zip Code

Email Address

Re: Trademark Infringement of RADIANCE IP LAW

Dear First Name:

We own the RADIANCE IP LAW[15] trademark, including U.S. Trademark Registration No. 5260168 for the same. Since October 2015, we have used the RADIANCE IP LAW trademark in connection with legal services.

It has recently come to our attention that, despite our exclusive rights in the RADIANCE IP LAW mark, your business is using RADIENCE for legal consulting and training services. We believe your use infringes on our ownership of the RADIANCE IP LAW mark. As owner of the RADIANCE IP LAW mark, we have an obligation to prevent infringement. Because you are using the identical or similar mark on the identical or similar products and/or services, we believe your use of RADIENCE has caused confusion or is likely to cause customer confusion.

While the purpose of this letter is to open a dialogue between us, we are prepared to take any and all legal action necessary to protect our trademark rights. You have infringed on our registered trademark. You must immediately cease and desist any and all use of RADIENCE, including similar variations, and confirm that you have ceased all use and will not use RADIENCE, or anything similar, in the future by responding in writing to this letter by [deadline].

If you have any questions about this letter, please contact me.

Sincerely,

[Signature]

_____

First Name and Last Name
Title
Company Name

---

15 Include your registered trademark here and throughout the letter. Also reference the other party's infringing trademark.

Intellectual Property Comparison Chart

Type	Trademark	Copyright	Patent	Trade Secret
Scope of Protection	A trademark protects your brand. It also identifies and distinguishes the source of the goods and services of one party from others.	A copyright protects original works of authorship.	A patent protects inventions.	A trade secret protects business information that has value in secrecy.
Examples	Business names Product or service names Slogans Logos	Written materials Music Artwork Videos Books Photographs Software coding	Products Processes	Recipes Formulas Compilations Methods Techniques Processes
Method of Protection	Actual commercial use and federal registration with the U.S. Patent and Trademark Office	Automatically upon creation, but a federal registration from the U.S. Copyright Office is required to file a lawsuit	Federal registration with the U.S. Patent and Trademark Office	Secrecy and a nondisclosure and confidentiality agreement

Intellectual Property Audit

You're probably sitting on an IP goldmine, and you don't even realize it. There is so much money you're leaving on the table by not identifying and capitalizing on your IP. This audit is a roadmap to your hidden treasures. Let's get started!

Step 1: Identify Your IP

Start digging through your business for all the intellectual property assets you have — both obvious and subtle. Compile a comprehensive list so that you know exactly what's there. Don't worry — you can determine its value at a later date.

Trademark — protects your brand (e.g., business name, product/service name(s), course name(s), book series name(s), podcast name, slogan, logo, app icon)

Identify your trademarks:

_____

_____

_____

_____

Copyright — protects your content (e.g., songs, artwork, designs, blog posts, courses, movies, photos, software coding, books, guides, manuals, recipes, worksheets, info-graphics, guides, templates, videos, training materials, presentations, strategy plans, frameworks)

Identify your copyrights:

_____

_____

_____

_____

Patent — protects your inventions (e.g., products, processes)

Identify your patents:

_____

_____

_____

_____

_____

Trade Secret — protects your secret business information (e.g., recipes, formulas, compilations, methods, techniques, processes)

Identify your trade secrets:

_____

_____

_____

_____

_____

Step 2: Prioritize Your IP

You're going to prioritize your list of items from Step 1. Identify your top 5 assets that you can capitalize on quickly.

Consider these questions when evaluating:

- Which do you love and treasure the most?
- What jumps out as having the most profit potential?
- What jumps out as being the most marketable?
- What jumps out as something you've been asked for over and over again?

Consider potential joint venture, licensing, and/or strategic partnership opportunities. Think about providing an additional way for people to benefit from your knowledge at various price points. Developing your IP allows you to extend your reach to different segments of people who need your expertise, but maybe can't afford to work with you one-on-one or people who want a technical or physical solution (like an app, journal, or course).

List Your Top Five Assets:

_____

_____

_____

_____

_____

Step 3: Protect Your IP

You must protect your IP *before* you can monetize and profit from it.

BONUS:

Identify Your Biggest Liabilities *(check the box only if the answer is YES)*

- ☐ I have previously worked with or spoken to an attorney regarding my intellectual property.
- ☐ Before choosing a new company name, product/service name, slogan, and/or logo, I perform research and due diligence on the U.S. trademark databases and search engines to ensure that I am not violating or infringing third party trademark rights.
- ☐ Before using any third-party photographs or content, I first obtain permission from the owner.
- ☐ I have federally registered all trademarks with the U.S. Patent and Trademark Office.

☐ I have federally registered all valuable copyrights, such as music, books, poems, designs, etc. with the U.S. Copyright Office.

☐ I have federally registered all patents with the U.S. Patent and Trademark Office.

☐ I use trademarks and trademark designations (TM or ®) appropriately on all products and materials.

☐ I include copyright © notices on all company-owned content, including but not limited to websites, publications, artwork, software, etc.

☐ I have procedures in place to ensure that my company, including its employees and contractors, does not infringe on third party intellectual property rights.

☐ I have procedures and agreements in place to protect company trade secrets.

☐ I have appropriate IP ownership, indemnification, and confidentiality language in all company contracts, and I have all employees, contractors, and consultants sign those contracts.

☐ I have thoroughly reviewed opportunities for licensing IP to third parties.

Each unchecked box is a business liability.

Acknowledgments

I extend my appreciation and thanks to the Radiance IP Law team, who has supported me throughout this book-writing journey and beyond...

To photography genius, Amanda Ghobadi, of The Branding Babe, who worked her magic in the beautiful photographs on the front and back covers of this book...

To book writing coach extraordinaire, Linda Griffin, of Grass Roots Marketing Systems LLC, who guided me through the entire book-writing process...

To anyone and everyone who has ever supported or encouraged me, thanks for inspiring me to strive for excellence so that I can help others do the same.

Bibliography

"50+ Eye-Opening Branding Statistics - 2020 Edition." 2019. SmallBizGenius. August 2, 2019. https://www.smallbizgenius.net/by-the-numbers/branding-statistics/.

"ENERGY STAR | The Simple Choice for Energy Efficiency." n.d. ENERGY STAR | The Simple Choice for Energy Efficiency. Accessed October 12, 2020. https://www.energystar.gov/.

"Headings of International Trademark Classes, TMEP 1401.02(a), October 2018." n.d. TMEP. Accessed October 12, 2020. https://tmep.uspto.gov/RDMS/TMEP/current#/current/TMEP-1400d1e1.html.

"How to Claim Acquired Distinctiveness under Section 2(f) | USPTO." n.d. United States Patent and Trademark Office. Accessed October 12, 2020. https://www.uspto.gov/trademark/laws-regulations/how-claim-acquired-distinctiveness-under-section-2f-0.

"The Ultimate Guide to Choosing a Brandable Name for Your Startup • Domain.Me Blog." 2018. Domain .ME Blog. January 19, 2018. https://domain.me/the-ultimate-guide-to-choosing-a-brandable-name-for-your-startup/#:~:text=Namely%2C%20studies%20show%20that%2077%25%20of%20customers%20make,a%20headache%2C%20you%E2%80%99ll%20ask%20someone%20for%20an%20Aspirin.

"TMEP § 803.05 (Address of Applicant)." n.d. TMEP. Accessed October 12, 2020. https://tmep.uspto.gov/RDMS/TMEP/Oct2016#/Oct2016/TMEP-800d1e419.html.

"TMEP § 1101 (Bona Fide Intention To Use the Mark In Commerce)." n.d. Accessed October 12, 2020.

"TMNG | IDML." n.d. TMNG | IDML Main Entry. Accessed October 12, 2020. https://idm-tmng.uspto.gov/id-master-list-public.html.

"Trademark Fee Information | USPTO." n.d. United States Patent and Trademark Office. Accessed October 12, 2020. https://www.uspto.gov/trademark/trademark-fee-information.

About the Author

Radiance W. Harris, Esq. is an award-winning trademark attorney, speaker, and author. As the founder and managing attorney of Radiance IP Law, she helps small and emerging businesses protect, monetize, and leverage profitable brands with trademarks. She has successfully represented startups and multinational corporations across diverse industries. Previously, she worked at the world's largest law firm representing Fortune 200 brands.

During her extensive career, Radiance has been widely recognized as a thought leader in the intellectual property law field. Her accolades include Maryland Rising Stars for Intellectual Property by Super Lawyers, Washington, D.C. Rising Stars for Intellectual Property by Super Lawyers, and Nation's Best Advocates: 40 Lawyers Under 40, to name a few. She has also been featured as a legal expert in a variety of publications, including Forbes.

With highly-specialized knowledge and expertise in trademark law, Radiance knows how to simplify complex legal topics and present them in entertaining, practical, and understandable ways to non-legal minds.

Made in the USA
Middletown, DE
20 March 2021